THE SECRET LAW OF ATTRACTION

Master The Power of Intention

BY KATHERINE HURST

THE LAW OF ATTRACTION.com™

D0910517

Published by Greater Minds Ltd
London, United Kingdom

ISBN: 978-0-9562787-8-4

Catalogue Data:
The Secret Law of Attraction - Master The Power of Intention

1. Law Of Attraction   2. Self Help   3. Personal Development

Greater Minds Ltd provides books at trade and other special
discounts to use as premiums, sales promotions, or for use in
training programmes.

If you are unable to order this book from your local bookseller,
you may order directly from the publisher.

Website: www.greaterminds.com

If you would like to share this book with others then you can
direct them to our website www.thelawofattraction.com/book
where it can be downloaded for free.

Printed in Great Britain by
Createspace

CONTENTS

CHAPTER ONE

Introduction

f you've recently heard about the Law of Attraction and wondered whether it can work, I'm here to tell you that my own amazing experiences are proof that it can! While I have a life of unparalleled happiness and abundance now, I can assure you that it wasn't always this way. Just a few years ago, I woke up every single day feeling flat, bored and resentful. Sure, I had a job and a safe place to live, so I knew I was lucky in a certain sense. However, I couldn't say I was *happy*. My work was soulless, my emotional life was empty, and my relationships were shallow. To make matters worse, I really couldn't see how I would ever be able to change things. I wanted better for myself, but I thought there was just no way out. If this scenario sounds painfully familiar to you, I want you to know that there are tools out there that can offer you the chance to transform your way of being.

So many people are held back by limiting beliefs that stifle their true potential and leave them feeling frustrated or alone. Hear this: it's not your fault that you have these limiting beliefs! They're actually passed down through generations in more than one way. For one thing, they can be transmitted through social interaction in your family, and you may have already given some thought to how your parents and your culture have imbued you with a certain level of negativity. To add to this, however, cutting edge science is now showing us that limiting beliefs can also be passed down genetically. Leading researchers in Atlanta have conducted studies showing that when mice associated the smell of cherry blossom with experiencing a small electric shock, they become hyper-sensitive to that smell. This is the astounding apart: when these mice breed, they pass this anxiety down to their offspring! In other words, mice who have never experienced a single electric shock still fear the scent of cherry blossom because their parents did. Brain imaging studies show that the offspring mice literally have different receptors in their brains. In light of these discoveries, consider that you too might be carrying genetically inherited fears and limiting beliefs that you got directly from your parents. While these beliefs have nothing to do with *your* experiences, they're still holding you back.

The great news is that learning how to work with the Law of Attraction can take you down the fruitful path of rewriting your belief system, counteracting the limiting beliefs you have inherited. And when you're free, you can finally use all of your untapped potential to change your life script. Whether you're looking for love, money, an amazing career or simply a healthier mental life, my approach to the Law of Attraction gives you an immediate advantage over those who are still blindly struggling with a negative burden unwittingly passed down through generations. If you have the intention to change the way your mind works and start vibrating on a more positive frequency, I have every confidence you can succeed.

Are you wondering how you can possibly change the world around you just by changing the way you think? When you first hear about the Law of Attraction, it's entirely natural to think it sounds too good to be true. That was my first thought too, if I'm honest! Nevertheless, as fanciful as it might sound, the truth is the Law of Attraction really can work. I used it to transform a life full of drudgery and boredom into one bursting with inspiration, financial abundance and true happiness—and I'm here to tell you that you can choose to do the same. While the Law of Attraction can initially sound cryptic and obscure, once you develop an understanding of the theory behind it, the key teachings can be boiled down into some wonderfully practical skills and techniques. It's all about learning new ways to set powerful intentions and sustain those intentions over time.

So, if you've recently discovered the Law of Attraction and want to start learning more about how you can use this amazing tool to improve your life, this is the book that can really change things for you. Through years of working to better understand how people can manifest their dreams, I've learned how to use straightforward language and concepts to explain and demonstrate use of the Law of Attraction. The core ideas are deeply intuitive, and I don't believe they should be shrouded in mystery. I'll walk you through an explanation of what the Law of Attraction really is, and then I'll explain how you can put it to work in your everyday life. By offering concrete tips and practical techniques you can immediately start using, I'll help you see how you can finally build the life you've always dreamed of having. I hope you enjoy this unique opportunity to learn and grow!

CHAPTER TWO

How the Law of
Attraction Works

f you think that the Law of Attraction is something that you need to work to bring into your life, you're wrong. It's *already* influencing you, every single day! When I talk about using the Law of Attraction, what I mean is harnessing, influencing and directing something that's already a live part of your life. In a nutshell, the presence of the Law of Attraction means that you magnetically attract whatever you focus on. So, if your mind is clogged up with negative thoughts, then it should be no surprise that somehow you end up feeling unsatisfied, bored, or like you just can't achieve your goals. Meanwhile, unconscious parts of your mind are also playing a role in what you attract, which explains why some individuals who *think* they're positive people still seem to attract negative things. This is where that research on mice and cherry blossoms really becomes relevant; your negativity might be flying completely under your radar, because some of it is preprogrammed into your genetic and neurological makeup! And that negativity can undermine you at every stage.

Think of a time when things just didn't seem to be going right for you. For example, maybe you were applying for jobs and never being called in for interviews, or perhaps you kept going on dates with people who turned out to be absolutely nothing like your ideal partner. What was your mindset around the time that these events were happening? You might be tempted to say "Well, of course I desperately *wanted* to have a successful career/ an amazing romance." However, did you believe that you could really achieve that goal? And if part of you did believe it, wasn't there an underlying sense of fear, or even a stronger, more forceful voice in your head saying that disaster was going to strike? When we want something, our limiting beliefs come out of the woodwork to produce frightening thoughts and images representing our failure. The resulting negativity only attracts more negativity; this is the Law of Attraction working in precisely the way you *don't* want it to work.

One of the most common limiting beliefs is this: "I'll never get what I want." While this type of limiting belief sometimes comes from bad experiences you've had, it is also commonly part of a self-fulfilling prophecy. In other words, even though you know what you want, you don't believe you can get it. As a result, you *don't* get it, and you continue to believe that you can't get what you want, and on the vicious cycle goes. I know it can feel scary to think about committing to a particular goal, but this lack of commitment is what can really stop you from having a better life! If you think back to areas where you have succeeded, you'll see how genuine commitment can make an incredible difference.

For example, try to think now of a contrasting case from your past. Cast your mind back to something that makes you feel proud, no matter how big or small. Maybe it was a great exam grade in school, an amazing presentation you gave at work, or a competition you won. When you think back to this instance, you should be able to see a very different mindset from the one occurring in cases of failure and disappointment. Perhaps you have people around you, offering encouragement and support, or perhaps you just focused in on a gut feeling of positivity and confidence. In contrast to the above, this sort of case shows the Law of Attraction has sometimes worked well for you, even when you didn't know its name! As you can see when you look back over your life history so far, the Law of Attraction is constantly in the background, and the attitude you that you take is one of the driving forces that can control what you attract every day. Once you learn techniques that inspire massive energy shifts towards the positive, you create opportunities for even greater possibilities.

Before I had my own chance encounter and the breakthrough moment that led me to start becoming an advanced user of the Law of Attraction, I was very much in the negative state of mind I just described when trying to get you to think of your own examples. I just couldn't shake my feelings of apathy, worthlessness and sadness, but because I also felt the yearning for a better life, I assumed that I was fully *wanting* that better life. In truth, I was only in the right headspace to start taking advantage of the Law of Attraction when I moved on to a more positive mindset (where the focus was on what I believed *could be* rather than on what I believed I *currently lacked*). That's the mindset I want to help you get into as well! Although it will involve lots of fun exercises and techniques that tap into your intuition, it starts with understanding the real power of the heart. After we look at the heart's role in the Law of Attraction, we can start jumping right into the types of exercises I promised at the outset.

CHAPTER THREE

The Power of the Heart

Mastering the power of intention becomes a lot easier once you start to give more weight to your *heart* and see how it influences every part of your life. While the mind is an amazing tool that you'll need all throughout your Law of Attraction journey, you need the input of the heart as well. Many of us are very practiced at shutting the heart down, until we're almost numb to the intuitions it can provide. However, there are good, science-based reasons to believe that the heart is more important than you know.

HeartMath Research on the Heart as a "Brain"

At the HeartMath Institute Research Center, scientists are investigating the physiology behind the heart's connection with the brain. They want to know how the heart impacts on the way we perceive things, how we feel, the way we process information, and the state of our health. There are fascinating questions to be answered about love, the ways in which stress influences the autonomic nervous system, and whether our immune systems are more connected to the heart than we previously thought.

While the Research Center's work is ongoing, one thing they've already uncovered is how important *heart rhythms* are to our emotional lives. In particular, how the variability of the heart rate can be linked to feelings of stress and unhappiness. When you're upset in some way, it leads to disorder in the heart's rhythms, impacting on parts of the nervous system that then create a sense of "disharmony" that's felt all throughout the body. The upside of this research is the discovery that when you feel positive emotions, there is harmony and coherence in the nervous system and in heart rhythm patterns.

What does this scientific research on the heart mean for your use of the Law of Attraction? Well, here's the most exciting discover so far: when you learn new ways to boost coherence in rhythmic patterns of heart rate variability, the heart appears to influence perception, awareness, emotion and intelligence in very positive ways. The heart is actually a kind of "brain" in itself; it organizes, processes and sorts information in ways that influence everything from your cognitions to your hormone balances. And the methods you can use to achieve this coherence are often very similar to the types of techniques I advocate when using the Law of Attraction. So, there are two major lessons to draw here. The first is that by influencing the heart, using Law of Attraction techniques influences your *body* in a measureable way, improving your emotional state and enhancing your perception. The second is that knowing the power of your heart can help you better understand what might be holding you back from using the Law of Attraction, as it's not just what's in your mind that matters.

Introduction to the Intention Point

The Heart Math studies is linked to another subject that's particularly important when you're trying to master the power of intention. Now that you can see that the heart and mind are equally powerful and vital parts of you, give some thought to times when you have *prioritized* one over the other. After all, who hasn't been pulled between the head and the heart, when choosing between a logically sound option and a seemingly irrational one that inspires passion.

If you're going to make the best of working with the Law of Attraction, you'll need to find a way to access the halfway point *between* the heart and mind. This is what I call the *Intention Point*. It's the absolute epicenter of your energy, and it influences every part of you, and it's the sacred part of you that the Universe responds to. When your heart and mind aren't on the same page, this Intention point is out of balance. As a result, it sends out confusing, mixed signals to the Universe, and can make it harder to manifest the things you desire. Many people also report links between an unbalanced Intention Point and feelings of lethargy, low mood and "stuckness."

So, how do you know if you're dealing with this type of imbalance, so that you can take steps to send out a more coherent message that mirrors your deepest wishes? You can learn how to locate your Intention Point within your own body, which is something I've learned to do in a straightforward, streamlined way. I'm so excited about it that I've made it the central focus of my breakthrough program "Origins." Depending on the position in which you find your Intention Point, you can learn a lot about your internal state and what needs to change. For example, some positions indicate you are bound by negative energy (which can cause tiredness and melancholy), while others suggest you actually have too *much* energy (leading to anxiety in some cases). And when you know where your

Intention Point is, you can learn exercises that shift it to a place of balance that promotes a better connection between the heart and mind.

For now, I'm just telling you about the Intention Point so that you can be more conscious of the connection between your heart and mind. This should be in the background all the way through your exploration of exercise and techniques in this book, and it's what will help you master the power of intention in a way that primes you to become more effective at manifestation than you've ever been before. However, that further work is something you can turn your full focus towards, sensing and adapting, once you've learned more of the basic principles of the Law of Attraction. To that end, let's look at how you can start using the Law of Attraction *today*!

To learn more about the Intention Point and my Origins program, please go to:

www.thelawofattraction.com/learn-about-origins/

CHAPTER FOUR

Mastering The Power Of Your Intentions

There are lots of specific exercises you can do in order to start improving your ability to use the Law of Attraction immediately. All of them can be started this moment without hesitation, and I'll explain why each of them is intimately related to the concepts of intention and manifestation. As a bonus, very few of them require any props, and those that suggest the use of objects can usually be acquired without much expense. Let's start with some of the techniques that are cornerstones of my preferred approach to the Law of Attraction.

Practicing Creative Visualization

Even if you already know a little bit about how visualization is used by proponents of the Law of Attraction, you may not know just how much research there is out there to support the power of visualization. People who may not even ever have encountered the Law of Attraction are using visualization to make concrete improvements in performance. In particular, many athletes swear that they are more likely to triumph if they take the time to see their success in their mind's eye. Curious about this apparent link, psychologists have instigated neuroimaging studies in an effort to find out what actually goes on in the brain when visualizing occurs. What has been found is that when you rehearse skills visually in your mind's eye, neural firings are sparked in the muscle, and you create or strengthen a kind of internal blueprint that guides you towards success in the relevant area. For example, skiers who were studied experienced just the same electrical impulses and muscle patterns when visualizing as they did when they were actually skiing out in the world! So, in a very real sense, when you visualize something you are actually *experiencing* it, believing in it, and (in Law of Attraction terms) sending out vibrations that may enhance manifestation.

In addition, any type of mindfulness exercise has the potential to influence you on other beneficial neurological levels, meaning it might also help to get rid of of some of those in-built limiting beliefs we were thinking about earlier. Some scientific research even shows that mindfulness work can reshape and change the brain, even at the level of size. It's possible for positive adaptations like better memory, increased capacity to deal with stress, and enhanced compassion to develop. Neuroscientists sometimes talk about the capacity that mindfulness has to encourage people to take charge of their own happiness, and I believe that part of this power comes from the link between positive mindfulness exercises and the Law of Attraction. Some of the breathing techniques you can do before delving into your visualizations count as a type of mindfulness, so there is the possibility of benefiting in so many ways when you adopt these daily techniques!

Where and When to Visualize

First, let's think about the kind of place in which it might be easiest to really focus in on a visualization. You might already have a setup in mind, but if you don't, then I encourage you to think about the following factors when picking out the right place to visualize:

- It's vital that your visualization space not be distracting, noisy, or likely to be disturbed during your process. You'll benefit from somewhere that's quiet, peaceful, and has a door that can be closed (if not locked). It's also worth considering giving any other people in the house (kids included) a heads up that you're going to need a bit of quiet time and don't want to be interrupted unless there's an emergency.

- You'll also need to be very comfortable, especially if you plan to make your visualizations longer than ten minutes. Any pain or discomfort in your body can take away from the positivity you build through visualizing, so plan this in advance. Is there a special chair that would work best? Are you more comfortable sitting on a cushion? Would lying down be preferable (e.g. if you have chronic back pain)?

- While you don't need to have any particular decoration in the area or place any specific furniture there, it's worth considering ways to create a peaceful, happy mood. For example, could you add flowers? Could you put up an inspirational picture? Could you visualize near other things you've been creating as part of your Law of Attraction work, such as a Dream Board (which we'll come back to later)?

- Once you've got a good idea of where you're going to be doing your visualizations, the next step is to consider *when* you'd get the most out of visualizing. I think it's a fantastic idea for you to do it on a daily basis, and that's what I do, but it's more a matter of deciding what time of day gets the best results for you. Here are some advantages and potential disadvantages to choosing different times:

- Visualizing in the morning gets your mind onto a great track for the day ahead. By focusing in on your goals and your positive feelings about those goals, your energy immediately starts being directed towards productive activity. However, visualizing in the morning does require getting up a bit earlier, so if you're already pressed for time (e.g. because of young children or very early shift work) then you may not be so keen on this idea!

- Visualizing in your lunch break (if you work) or around your dinner time can be useful if you've been an environment that has the potential to sap your energy (such as a job that isn't the ideal one you wish for). On the other hand, these can also be busy times of day for some people, and I wouldn't encourage you to cram in a rushed visualization if you don't feel you can fully commit to it.

- Finally, visualizing before going to bed can lead to some amazing, inspiring dreams that give you new ideas about ways to manifest a better future. It also ensures that you go to sleep feeling calm and emotionally at peace, which could improve sleep quality and also get rid of any negative thoughts that might have been creeping in during the day. That being said, I've heard some people say that they accidentally fall asleep during night time visualizations, or that they feel they don't get the full benefit of the energy shift because they're not actually living everyday life directly after visualizing!

If one of these options doesn't immediately stand out to you, don't worry about it at all. Simply start with one (let your gut guide you towards which one to start with!), and then try out each of the options until you get a sense of the one that's right for you. Most people find it pretty obvious after just a few attempts.

How to Visualize

As I noted above, you can get yourself into the right headspace for a visualization technique (and boost the extent to which you reap the benefits of mindfulness!) by starting out with some basic breathing exercises. Really, all you need to do to prepare is to spend about 3-5 minutes sitting comfortably, and focusing on your breathing. Inhale through your nose, then out through your mouth, and make a conscious effort to slow down your respiration rate. As you may know, the objective here is to clear your mind as much as you can. While it won't be possible to stop thoughts, ideas and commitments from popping into your mind (especially during your first few attempts!), the trick is to *let them float by*. So, if you catch yourself starting to wonder what you should pick up at the store later, don't panic! Just turn your attention back to your breathing, leaving that question unanswered.

After a period of deep breathing, your mind should ideally feel calm and relaxed, while your limbs and muscle should be loose, with all the tension slowly draining away. You're now primed to build up your visualization!

So, think of whatever you want to manifest, whether it's that job, partner, overflowing bank account, great home or amazing career. Now, slowly and carefully build up the most detailed image you possibly can. I've known lots of people who've tried to create visualizations that are too temporally expansive, and I want to suggest you keep your mental image *time-limited*. In other words, don't try to visualize days, weeks or years of your dream life! Stick to a moment: the kind of moment that makes your heart fill with joy and gives you the sense that anything is possible. For example, if you're looking for love, it could be a first kiss with a perfect partner that you visualize, or it could be the peace and intimacy of falling asleep together in bed at night. Focus in on every little detail of this image, and really try to live it. That's what creative visualization is all about.

When you've visualized for 10-15 minutes (though everyone's ideal time limit is different, so you should feel free to experiment), slowly open your eyes and come back to the room. Feel the certainty, happiness, positivity and energy in your gut, and try to take it with you wherever you're going (whether that's to work, bed, on a date or somewhere else entirely).

The Importance of Perspective

How have you been visualizing so far? If I had to bet, I'd say that you do it from a first person perspective. In other words, you probably see through your own eyes in the visualization, and imagine your environment around you. Although this might well be the best place to start and is certainly effective in its own right, it's well worth considering the possibility of doing creative visualizations from a *third person* perspective. So, instead of seeing through your eyes, you watch *yourself* doing the things you want to do.

Remember the athletes I mentioned earlier, who swore by visualization as a way to enhance their likelihood of success in sport? Well, many of them say that what improves their skills most of all is this type of type person visualization, where the image in their mind's eye is of *themselves*. However, I hasten to add that I don't think you should be locked into to any one type of perspective when you visualize. As with many Law of Attraction techniques, it's all about feeling your way to a version of the technique that feels right for *you*. Try a few approaches, and see what seems to provide the best results in your life!

So, you've now received a primer on how to visualize, which is arguably the most important skill of all! If you make a habit of visualizing every day, what you're doing is staying connected to your intention, and this kind of constant, positive focus can really start to change your life. Even without the ability to locate your Intention Point on a physical level (that will come later in your journey), you'll be doing things to shift it in a meaningful way.

The Dream Check Exercise

For this exercise, you can download the handy printable, blank check that I provide in my Law of Attraction Tool Kit! The basic notion behind the dream check is simple but powerful; it's another way to keep your heart and mind focused on what you want to manifest, instead of what you think you don't currently have. It's designed especially for those who are looking for financial abundance, and it's a classic Law of Attraction tool. Broadly speaking, it's a kind of visualization tool, and it encourages you to feel and think things that influence your energy by bring it in line with your desires.

The dream check looks like a regular check, all you need to do is print it, write your name down next to "pay" and then choose a sum that you'd like to receive! Think big, be ambitious, and allow yourself to feel fantastic about the idea of abundance. Keep it on you or near you, and look at it at regular intervals.

To learn more about the Intention Point and my Origins program, please go to:

www.thelawofattraction.com/learn-about-origins/

Designing Affirmations

You may already be familiar with the idea of using affirmations or positive mantras, whether through their appearance in pop culture or via previous material on the Law of Attraction. If you're not aware, an affirmation is basically a succinct, positive statement designed to lift your mood and keep your mind in tune with your goals. So, you can see why it might be a useful tool when you're trying to stay upbeat and confident as you work to master the power of intention and attract what you desire!

In my experience, the affirmations that resonate at the deepest levels are the ones that you design yourself. There tends to be a power and authenticity to your own words that is rarely captured by simply adopting something else's affirmations. However, it can be very useful to use "template" affirmations and then tweak them to your own purposes (especially if you've never done anything like this before). First, I'll outline the approach I use to come up with affirmations from scratch, and then I'll show you some template affirmations that you can adjust to your heart's content! Finally, I'll suggest how you can use affirmations in everyday life.

Creating Affirmations

Start by finding a quiet space where you won't be disturbed, just as you would for a visualization session. Grab a pen and a notepad, and make sure you're sitting comfortable. Next, focus your mind on the goal that is most important to you. How might you express your full belief that it's possible to reach that goal, and that you are in fact already on your way? Letting your intuition guide you, write down at least 10 short sentences without "filtering" any of your thoughts. Nothing is too silly, or too grand. When you have your list, let your heart guide you to just 1-3 of the affirmations that really hit home.

Adjusting Template Affirmations

Here are a few of the affirmations that have worked well for me or others I know. I've chosen ones that link up with some of the most common themes that crop up when people are using the Law of Attraction, but you can tweak them to make them more in line with any other goal you have too!

Love:

- "I am ready to meet the trustworthy, loving partner who is coming my way."

- "I'm excited, happy and ready to meet my match."

- "I'm going to have a great time on this date, no matter the outcome."

- "I am open and ready to receive the love I deserve."

- "I am beautiful and desirable.

- "I am magnetic, fun and sexy."

Financial abundance:

- "I can afford everything I need, without worry or stress."

- "I attract financial abundance wherever I go."

- "I am on the path to gain more wealth every day."

Physical change:

- "I have the strength to stick to this diet/fitness plan."

- "I am becoming healthier and more energetic every day."

- "I have the power to develop the body I deserve."

Social growth and confidence:

- "I am an attractive, vibrant person, and people will respond to this."

- "The only opinion that really matters if my own."

- "I trust myself to know what's best for me in life."

- "I am capable and confident."

- "I show my best self to others and will attract positivity wherever I go."

Career success:

- "Everyone sees I am valuable, talented and creative."

- "I am ready for great opportunities, and others will recognize this."

- "I am successful and deserving of a job that I love."

- "Every moment brings me closer to doing the work I've always wanted."

These are just handy references to get you started.

You can see more sample affirmations in my free Law of Attraction Tool Kit. Just go to:

www.thelawofattraction.com/book-resources/

Ways to Use Affirmations in Everyday Life

The standard way to use affirmations is to say them out loud in a clear, steady voice, focusing your mind on the key message they communicate. Some people like to say them into a mirror, holding their own gaze as they do so. Others prefer to close their eyes and really tune into their words. However, I'd also encourage you to think about alternative ways to connect with your chosen affirmations. For example, if you favor written communication over speaking, you might find that writing out your affirmations on a daily basis is a more powerful way to let them influence your mood. You can also write them onto large pieces of paper, and display them where you're most likely to see them at the right moment. For a weight loss affirmation, say, the right place might be the fridge! Meanwhile, an affirmation related to your work or dating life could be better located on your front door.

In addition, don't forget that you can use technology to your advantage here! When I've got a busy day ahead of me and I know that I need a little bit of extra help to stay in tune with my intentions, I like to set reminders that pop up on my smartphone. That way, I'm prompted to read my affirmations at particularly suitable times, reminding me of my most positive thoughts and dreams. You can also try recording your affirmations and listening to them through headphones during a commute. Be as creative and inventive as you like when you're working with affirmations. The only rule is that you should go with whatever makes you feel happiest and most connected with your vision of a better life!

Once again, the affirmations section of my Law of Attraction Tool Kit has further tips and tricks for using this type of approach in the most productive and enjoyable way. Meanwhile, in Origins, part of my goal is to help you understand the types of things that may be getting in the way of successful using affirmations. Further, if you're really into the idea of affirmations and find that they work well for you, you'll find that Origins helps you to delve more deeply into the idea of using affirmation-like exercises to overcome limiting beliefs (once they're identified and clarified).

Boosting Positivity

As you now know from reading this book so far, the Law of Attraction is constantly working, and what you invite into your life has so much to do with the general tenor of your thoughts and feelings. Consequently, in addition to arming yourself with the techniques and exercises that Law of Attraction experts encourage you to try, one of the best things you can do to is take small steps to try and vibrant on a more positive frequency, every day. When you think in a positive way, your positive thoughts just get stronger, more powerful and more entrenched. This, in turn, helps you increase your chances of achieving your goals. Here are some methods that might inspire you to find new ways to stay upbeat.

Keeping a Gratitude Journal (or Jar)

There's so much to be grateful for every day, but many of us are so busy worrying about the future or dwelling on the past that we take these little bursts of positivity for granted. One way to discourage this attitude is to find something that keeps you more anchored in the present. A gratitude journal can fit into even the busiest of lives; if you only have time to write down one sentence or a few bullet points every 2-3 days, you're still deliberately becoming more mindful and conscious of the things that inspire appreciation. Meanwhile, if you want to write something longer each day, then go for it! Some people also like to challenge themselves by focusing their gratitude log on a specific subject that they tend to ignore. For example, you might decide to write down only encounters with natural beauty if you think you tend to breeze through the world without "smelling the roses." Whether you want to record gratitude about all or just some parts of your existence, the idea is to look beyond the big things. So, while it is of course amazing to get a promotion, have a first kiss with a new date or master a skill, I'm talking about seeing the little moments that make life so textured. So, think of the way a meal smelled, the kindness of a stranger, or the extra hour you had in bed because of a delayed meeting.

An alternative to a gratitude journal is to use a jar. You may already have heard of this technique, as it's getting quite popular. The thought is that you write down things that make you feel grateful, then fold them up and put them a jar. Then, when your mood dips (or you just want to evaluate the past month or year), you can empty out the jar and rediscover all the reasons you have to be a positive, grateful person.

Spreading Gratitude

When people start getting the hang of the Law of Attraction, one of the things they often seem to notice is that others are responding to them in a new way. This is the pull of a positive mindset! When you're consciously trying to maintain a productive focus on feelings of confidence, happiness and determination, your behavior can be quite infectious. Although this change tends to happen all by itself, you can enhance it (and therefore ensure you're surrounded by even *more* powerful positivity) by finding new ways to spread gratitude and joy. Try saying "thank you" (sincerely!) at every suitable chance you get. Tell friends you appreciate them, verbally acknowledge the extra hours that diligent co-worker has put into your shared project, and be sure to thank the stranger who holds the door open for you. As you give out gratitude, you attract gratitude, and all this positive energy flowing around you will help you to master the power of intention.

Treating Yourself With Kindness

Another way to help yourself feel more positive every day is to consider how you can better facilitate self-care. When I worked in my soul-crushing job, I collapsed into bed every night feeling exhausted and sad, never really thinking about how I could bring a bit more light into my days. Once I started learning about the Law of Attraction, I got an increasing sense of just how important it was to play an active role in my own care. Here, for example, are little things you can consider fitting into your day if you want to create the kind of positive well-being that can help you vibrate on the right frequency to attract the things you want:

- Spend at least 30 minutes a day doing something just for pure pleasure or enjoyment. Whether it's reading a fiction book, playing a musical instrument, watching a favourite show or drinking a cup of green tea and enjoying a nice view, you may be surprised by how much even half an hour of this sort of time can change your mood.

- Take an indulgent bath, and focus on how it pleases all of your senses. Consider lighting some candles and creating a soothing atmosphere. Bonus points if it's a bubble bath, and if you take a glass of your favorite drink in with you! When you treat yourself like this, you send out a signal that you *value* yourself and believe you *deserve* the things you want.

- When you're asked to add something extra to your schedule, give yourself a moment to think about whether this thing will drain the last of your resources. If it would, then say "no" and don't feel guilty for a moment! If you deplete all of your resources, you lack the energy required to master the power of intention (potentially undermining your goals).

- In addition to practicing creative visualization, consider whether you might add a daily meditation or mindfulness exercise to your day. A relaxing meditative journey can put you in the focused, open state of mind you need to tackle the day ahead (or decompress after a tiring one). You can find lots of meditations online or through apps, and they're often geared towards relaxing stiff muscles, recentering yourself, and becoming more peaceful. This has obvious benefits for your mindset!

I could list dozens of ways to take care of yourself, of course, especially when you think about how important things like diet and exercise can be. However, what I've offered above is just a quick list of ideas to get you thinking. The message I'd like you to take away is that when you're good to yourself and believe it's warranted, you let the universe know that you have faith in your own worth—helping you use the Law of Attraction for positive developments. How exactly you choose to demonstrate your self-worth and self-compassion is up to you!

Learning Lessons

When you encounter setbacks (or things that *look* like setbacks), you can bolster your positivity by viewing these challenges as potential messages from the universe. These are messages that tell you something about how you can move closer to a happier future! If you're willing to really look at these difficult days, you'll often see a hidden gem of information that teaches you something very important. For example, the date you didn't enjoy can be seen as a way to further refine your visualization of an ideal partner. Meanwhile, if you don't feel you quite nailed that job interview the way you wanted to, make a list of skills you can acquire for next time. You may be surprised to find out that you excel in the next interview, and that the job turns out to be so much more satisfying than the other one you applied for!

The main suggested plan of action here is to tell yourself that you're going to find the silver lining every time, and look for positive interpretations.

Evaluating Relationships

A final approach I'd suggest you consider when aiming to boost positivity is evaluating your social ties to see where negativity might be seeping into your life. Are you surrounded by supportive people who truly enjoy celebrating your success, believe in your potential and are happy to give you as much as they take from you? If so, then you're naturally going to be more positive more of the time. If, however, you've been interacting with certain people who criticize you no matter what you do, experience jealousy when others do well, or don't offer you any support, it's so hard to stop this negativity from getting into your bones and interfering with your attempts to manifest your dreams!

Once I politely withdrew from the toxic influences in my own social circle, I quickly saw how much easier it was for me to be happy, confident, and focused on the goals I was trying to achieve through my use of the Law of Attraction. It's a cycle; when we're with positive people, we become more positive in response, and then become even more positive! The reverse is true if you're devoting energy to relationships that are less than the type you deserve.

Dream Boarding

If you're a visual learner who connects more with images than words, you're going to absolutely love the dream boarding technique. I offer a step-by-step guide to creating your first dream board in my Law of Attraction Tool Kit, but the premise is excitingly straightforward. All you need to do is get yourself a board (the bigger the better!), and cover it with the images that best represent the dream future you are aiming to manifest. Many people approach this task by cutting images from magazines and creating a collage of suitable photos. However, there are really no hard and fast rules here. As long as an image strikes the right chord with you, go right ahead and put it up there! If you're artistic, then you can even add your own drawings. And if you're *not* as keen on images as you are on words, you can cut those out or print them and attach them to your dream board as well (though this exercise tends to be more motivating if it includes at least some pictures).

You can get started today and begin creating your own dream board. My Law of Attraction Tool Kit has full instructions available here:

www.thelawofattraction.com/book-resources/

Once you've worked your way through my basic steps to creating a dream board, try to keep it around your environment without forcing yourself to look at it. If you get used to it being around and allow it to subtly, slowly have the potential to reshape your subconscious, you're way more likely to let dream boarding change those limiting beliefs I've mentioned so often in this book. However, do try to put it somewhere where you'll regularly encounter it in a positive context, even though you're goal is not to spend hours staring at it! Above your desk, where you get ready in the morning, or even on the wall by your bed are all places where it'll gradually become part of the furniture, quietly and consistently having the chance to keep your positive energy flowing towards your greatest goals.

Rejecting Your Comfort Zone

While you might think it sounds quite strange, people are often *scared* to succeed, and this is entwined with common limiting beliefs. For example, even if you like to fantasize about a world in which you have mastered the skills required to get your dream job, you might find that you actually avoid learning those skills because it's too frightening to think about obtaining them and then *failing* to get that amazing job you crave. As a result, sticking with a dull job and never trying to enhance your abilities feels safer.

As you can see, your limiting beliefs keep you in your comfort zone, which is what the cautious part of your mind wants (though your heart wants something else). While the comfort zone can feel very safe much of the time, it is also likely to ensure that you never meet your true potential. When you start to understand where those little critical voices inside your head came from (whether they're social or genetic), you can begin to rob them of their power. It's a task that takes time, and one I engage with more fully as part of my "Origins" program. However, take heart; there are things you can do that immediately start to lessen the power of your limiting beliefs, even before you tackle them at their very foundations.

One of the major steps you can take is to deliberately move out of your comfort zone, to prove those limiting beliefs wrong. You don't need to pack up and move to another country today, or quit your job on a whim. If you make little changes often enough, they can start to help reshape your belief system, showing you how much you *can* do (as opposed to keeping you trapped in fear of what you think you *can't* do). For example, you might say "yes" to a social event you would normally have shied away from, you might sign up for a class to start learning a new skill you've always coveted, or you could consider taking your first foray into online dating by setting up a profile. In addition, expose yourself to rousing success stories that prove how taking leaps can be the very thing that creates a better life! Moving out of your comfort zone not only helps to expand your notion of what you're capable of doing, but it also provides exciting opportunities for personal growth. Listen to your heart, and follow it instead of staying in the cage made by the most fearful parts of your mind!

CHAPTER FIVE

Manifestation Accelerator Techniques

At this stage, I think it's also appropriate to start sharing some of the more advanced techniques that I favour. These are mostly exercises that I started using further along my road to understanding the Law of Attraction, and ones that have tended to work best for people I've known when they had already mastered techniques like basic visualizations and affirmations.

Living "In the Knowing"

The idea behind this technique is to approach your life by doing things that you would do *if you had already achieved your dreams*. So, for example, you might phrase your affirmations in the present tense if you like this technique (e.g. using "I am so happy to have found love" instead of

"I know I will find love"). However, some people actually like to go beyond reshaping affirmations in this way and find it powerfully effective to write first-person, present tense accounts of what life is like when the goal has been achieved. To return to the love case again, you might write a full page description of what it's like to finally be in the relationship you craved, and express your appreciation for the fact this has occurred.

If living in the knowing feels like an approach that personally resonates with you (or if you've started using it and found it has a great impact), think about using the technique in an even more concrete way. This might involve actually buying a chair where your partner could sit with you in the evenings, or getting a brochure for the cars you aim to afford in a more abundant future.

Changing Your Home's Vibration

You have a unique vibration that can be influenced by all kinds of factors. Some are beyond your control, like sudden illness or injury, but others are subject to direct manipulation. One thing that's sure to impact on your vibration frequency is your home environment. Even if you have a hectic life, you eat, sleep and (hopefully) relax in your home at least some of the time, so take advantage of that fact and think about some ways to make your space more in tune with your intentions. Here are some suggestions that have worked well for me or people I know. Some of them are tailored to specific goals, while others are germane to just about anything you want to achieve.

- Try a few Feng Shui tricks to see if you can elicit positive emotions when you're in your home. In particular, experts caution that any dark colors tend to sap energy, and could even lower your mood. In contrast, nature-based shades like sunny yellow and the green of fresh grass can infuse you with energy, and keep you feeling upbeat. You don't have to decorate to get these kinds of benefits, either; just buying a green throw for your dark sofa or buying a few new yellow pillows could create the little boost you need.

- * Consider setting aside a specific shelf, table or other little area, and devoting this place to objects that connect you with your Law of Attraction goals. There are no rules here; just go with anything that makes you feel good and helps you focus on your increasing confidence in your success.

- Send out the signal that you're ready for a brand new, better way of being by getting rid of unwanted clutter in your home. Create as much space as you can; get rid of outdated clothes, worn out things, and objects that you just don't like. This process also helps you to move on from the past, symbolizing your ongoing process of leaving limiting beliefs and unproductive coping strategies behind. You may be surprised by how good you feel afterwards!

- You can take the above tip another step further by thinking about specific sources of negativity that might be in your home. For example, if you know that memories from your previous job or relationship are undermining your confidence about looking for a new one, get rid of some of the major things that evoke these memories! Stationary from your old office, company pens, letters from ex-partners... if you can bring yourself to scrap these things, you might find the vibration of your home seems to change in response. You can compromise by boxing items up and putting them out of sight if you struggle to fully abandon them.

Using Smells to Tap Into Your Heart

While you now realize that your heart can hold an unbelievable amount of power, you're also aware that sometimes you need to be a little covert when it comes to finding ways to *access* your heart. Your mind can throw up all kinds of defences, and things like changing your environment, rewriting your beliefs and practicing affirmations are all ways to get past those defenses and streamline your intentions. Like making amendments to your home, exposing yourself to certain smells can really help to keep your mood on track. I'd suggest using them as part of room sprays or acquiring ones for use with oil burners, but you can also approach a qualified aromatherapy practitioner to find out how to use topical treatments in a safe way (as some can interact with certain underlying medical issues). Here's a quick primer on six of my favorite essential oils when it comes to staying positive and determined.

- **Bergamot** is a good general purpose oil, because it's often recommended as being able to lift your spirits and give you a surge of extra energy. Very handy if you need a little extra help to stay upbeat during a long day!

- **Lavender** is famous for its ability to relax and sooth, so take advantage of this property if you feel any anxiety starting to develop in the pit of your stomach. Even if you're not that stressed, lavender is the kind of scent that slows the mind and gets you into a good place for meditation or visualization.

- **Orange oil** is one of the best scents for improving your focus, especially if you're trying to concentrate on taking in new information. It's known for helping you feel more awake, and it's also naturally uplifting.

- **Neroli** is said to increase creativity, so you can use it when you're trying to hone new skills, or when you're just about visualize your Law of Attraction goals.

- **Patchouli oil** has a musky smell that excites the senses and can make you feel attractive or confident—just the thing you need before a date. If you can get a perfume with patchouli in it, you may find the scent has a similar impact on your companion as well!

- **Rosemary** is at the center of some research buzz at the moment, thanks to a potential link with memory enhancement (that may be of use to those suffering from degenerative neurological disorders). It can also be of general use to anyone who wants to retain information, so it can give you a bit of reassurance when you're, say, preparing for a presentation or a job interview.

Thought Stopping

We'll soon turn to look at how you can turn negative thoughts into positive sources of energy, but first let's think about how you can halt negative thoughts in their tracks when they threaten to interfere with your Law of Attraction work. Although this technique isn't a long-term fix, it can be a kind of "band-aid" approach when you really need to get out of a negative headspace (e.g. in the lead up to a fantastic opportunity!). When you feel yourself thinking something critical or panicky, say "No!" in a loud and firm voice. If you're in a public space, you'll just have to say it internally, but make sure you still hear it loud and clear. You can also picture a bright red image of a stop sign, or hold your hand up in front of you as a physical gesture of defiance.

Advanced Visualization

When I first taught you about starting the visualization process, I put the focus on building a very clear, vivid *image* of what you want to accomplish. In particular, I suggested that you picture a specific moment related to that image: the image of a perfect partner, the phone call that tells you that you got the job, or the moment you slide into the seat of the new car you can finally afford. However, once you've got the basic visualization skillset down, I'd like you to start thinking about ways to get *all* of your senses as engaged as possible.

In other words, don't just ask yourself what it would *look like* to be in a moment associated with your most precious goals. Ask yourself what you would hear, taste, smell and feel. I'm talking as many details as you can possibly muster, from ambient noise to the texture of what you're wearing, the smell of your brand new office, the way your skin responds to an intimate touch, or the taste of the amazing meal you're eating at the dream destination you previously didn't have the resources to visit. Anything you can do to make this visualization as real as possible will help you to believe in your potential to live the life you want. And revisiting this visualization every single day will help to make sure you stay anchored in these happy, motivating feelings that are key to using the Law of Attraction for positive change.

The Focus Wheel

I love this technique, and think it's one of the most powerful ones you can employ when you're at the stage you've currently reached. It's all about really honing in on your specific intentions, and getting a more concrete sense of them. The name "Focus Wheel" comes from the fact that the exercise uses two circles (one inside the other) to create space for 12 different phases. For example, you might choose to focus on feelings of love writing down 12 things that make you feel appreciative (such as your wonderful home, the support you get from your loved ones, and so on). In particular, I like to choose things that I have, but which represent *things I want more of* in my life. So, if I was looking to manifest more confidence in my dating life, I would write about love I have for confidence I *already experience* in a certain arena, such as "I love how confidence and successful I feel when I'm with my best friend." Meanwhile, the centre of the circle is where you place your greatest intention, using as positive language as you can muster (a written version of living "as if").

You can learn more about this exercise and download a printable template that you can use to create your own Focus Wheel from scratch! I think it's a great idea to use your focus wheel as a source of affirmations, too; you can look at it a few times a day, read all the sentences out loud, and really devote energy to experiencing the associated emotions.

I wrote an article about this process on my blog and you can get your printable template here too:

www.thelawofattraction.com/add-oomph-to-your-intentions-with-a-focus-wheel/

Creating an Association

While you can create a strong association with any visualization, I decided to introduce the idea at this point because I think it's obviously going to be a more powerful technique when used in conjunction with the most vivid visualization you can muster. By "creating an association" what I mean is tethering your visualization to an object or a movement that allows you to immediately get back in touch with the amazing feelings that your mental image elicits. Some people like to hold a particular object (such as a stone or a piece of jewelry) during their creative visualization time, making a point of looking it or feeling its shape before and after the process. That way, if they carry the object with them, they can take it out and feel it or look at it any time that they feel a negative mindset creeping in or they just need an extra dose of positivity.

If you're particularly attracted to the idea of using

a stone, it's worth looking into the *meanings* of different stones. Some of them are traditionally said to be linked to particular themes or desires, many of which happen to resonate with common goals set when working with the Law of Attraction. I'll give you a few quick tips on popular stones before we move on to the idea of making associations using a *physical* cue (which requires no object at all).

Working with Stones

As with many choices, I think you should trust your gut and your intuition when picking out an object like a stone. When you get used to tapping into this intuitive side of yourself, you're accessing the heart, and (as you've already learned), the heart has such an important role to play when you're setting intentions. However, if you're not sure where to start, here are eight of the most commonly available stones, along with their traditional meanings and how they might connect with certain goals:

- **Agate** is associated with strength, courage and overcoming obstacles. So, whatever you aim to manifest, this stone can serve as a reminder that you have the power to do anything you set your mind to.

- **Clear quartz** can be thought of as the "master healer" and is a nice choice for anyone who wants a stone symbolizing the possibility of better health (whether mental, physical, or both).

- **Citrine** is frequently recommended as a symbol of abundance and prosperity, making it fit rather well with a desire for financial abundance *or* career success.

- **Imperial topaz** is an ancient remedy for a slow metabolism, so some people like to use it as representation of their desire to lose weight.

- **Rhodonite** is a stone of fertility, so you might draw comfort and positivity from its presence if you keep it nearby when you're trying to start or extend a family.

- **Rose quartz** is famously connected to the concepts of love and romance, so head straight for this one if finding a partner is on your mind (or, indeed, if improving a current relationship is your goal).

- **Smokey quartz** is sometimes called the "writer's block stone" which means you might be drawn to it if you're working towards a creative goal. However, it can also symbolize overcoming energy blocks more generally, so it's one to consider if you know you have a lot of limiting beliefs left to defeat.

- **Tiger eye**, like citrine, has long been thought of as a stone linked to wealth.

Remember, you can use any of these stones when doing your creative visualization process, and they can also easily be slipped into a pocket where you can touch them or simply notice their presence in potentially daunting situations like job interviews and first dates. The key is to try and build a strong connection between your positive thoughts and this object, eventually just seeing or touching the object is enough to kickstart the types of emotions that are connected to a greater potential for manifestation.

Working with Physical Cues

The alternative to using an object is using a physical cue, which has the benefit of being extremely subtle. So, you can "cue" yourself to feel fantastic about your manifestation goals at any time, no matter who is watching! You might touch your right knuckle every time you finish your visualization, or your left knee. Any touch or movement can work, in theory, so go with your gut. If you touch whatever area of your body you've chosen each and every single time you visualize, you can actually train your heart and mind to associate the particular touch with all the good feelings you crave. Then, eventually, you should be able to elicit those very same feelings without even having to go into a meditative state at all. I'm not saying you should ever quit your visualization sessions; rather, I'm just letting you know that you can harness some of their power *outside* that specific setting, and that it can be very comfortable and uplifting to do so.

Boosting Personal Magnetism

Now, another quick thought about expanding the goal of your visualizations before we move on to one of my favorite belief-changing exercises. While I definitely want to stress that I think it's smart to start out with a core visualization that you focus on every day, I sometimes do supplementary visualizations that have a wider ranging goal. Most commonly, I might choose to use the one I call the "Magnetism Visualization." It can help you to feel more confident about attracting what you want, and it's also potentially useful if you're going through a phase where you're not quite sure about a specific goal but know that you do want to manifest a better life.

As usual, just find a relaxing, quiet space where you're not going to be interrupted, and spend a few minutes focusing on maintaining slow, steady breathing (in order to calm your mind). Then, start to picture yourself throbbing with a positive, happy energy that has a magnetic quality. It's pulling good things towards you, and you can build up a feeling of what this would be like. I sometimes just focus on trying to create this feeling internally, but at other times I also picture my body radiating a brilliant golden light that draws others towards me. After just 10 minutes in this visualization, you can emerge feeling more inspired, focused and stimulated. If you didn't know what you wanted before you tried this visualization, you might now be struck by an intuition that helps to set you on the right track. I also like to use this type of visualization when I'm running a bit low on energy and need a quick boost to help me get going again!

The Positivity Switch

In the previous section, I told you about some of the basic techniques you can enact to start filling yourself with more positive energy and begin focusing on your true intentions. While all of those approaches can be powerful in their own right, the majority are concerned with attempting to generate *more* positivity or trying to ensure that you spend more time concentrating on good things (so that you attract more of what you really want). What I want to do now is share a technique that I find especially useful when I'm dealing with a very real sense of *negativity* (rather than a mere lack of positivity). As you'll see, moments of fear can actually be turned upside down, transforming them into amazing resources that propel you towards your goals.

I call this approach "flipping the Positivity Switch" and, if you're willing to fully commit to it, it can really help you put all that new knowledge about the power of the heart into action. This is a technique you can try when you're feeling anxious, confused, stressed out or downright afraid; it's a valuable alternative to just obsessing about your problem (which I believe really only gives fear and negativity even more power). It's all about moving into your fears, and facing them head on to diffuse them of their power and learn to lose them for good. All you have to do is answer the following questions, then take action based on your answers.

- **What's the worst that could happen?**
  Look you fear straight in the eyes, and
  think about what would *really* happen if
  it came to pass. When you do this, you'll
  frequently see that you actually have the

resources to overcome the feared outcome. This is a realization that can sap a lot of the threatening power the fear previously had!

- **What does your fear tell you about your goals?** Think about what your negative feelings can tell you about setting and achieving goals. If, say, you're terrified that you'll be stuck in your job forever, that's a sign that you can set a goal of finding a career opportunity that might better meet your needs. Once you have outlined this goal, focus on that empowering, progressive idea and not on the idea of fear.

- **What would life be like if this fear was irrelevant?** Armed with your new goal, set out to imagine how your future could make that old fear totally irrelevant. So, to return to the above example, you might visualize how worrying about a dead-end job will just no longer matter when you're in a fulfilling new occupation. Like we explored in the previous chapter, it's good to pick a particular time and visualize at that same time each day. Use all your new skills to make this visualization astoundingly vivid!

- **How can you make your goal a reality?**
  Now that you know what your goal is and
  you know exactly how it would look and feel
  to achieve it, devote energy and excitement
  to finding ways to start living that goal
  right away. Make lists, check things off, do
  something to maximize progress every day,
  and let yourself feel joy as you do so!

- **How can you stay positive?** Once you've
  flipped the positivity switch, you've already
  made a real change for the better. However,
  the old fear might start to creep back in,
  and if it does then remind yourself that you
  know how to refocus your mind by using that
  amazing visualization you've created, and
  the concrete outline of steps you're already
  taking. In addition, figure out a "first-aid kit"
  of things that instantly improve your mood.
  Whether it's a specific song, a long walk,
  exercise or a luxurious bath, keep those
  things on tap to help rebalance your mood if
  fear begins to resurface.

There's plenty you can do to supplement the Positivity Switch exercise, and the above just represents the basic outline. When you're ready to move onto more complex and far-reaching versions of techniques like his one, my "Origins" program could be a useful resource for you. To learn more please go to:

www.thelawofattraction.com/learn-about-origins/

CHAPTER SIX

Looking to the Future

What I've offered you in this book is what I consider to be a primer for using the Law of Attraction. There are certain basic ideas and approaches that are crucial to taking those first steps (in terms of both understanding and action), and I've enjoyed sharing those with you in the way that I wish someone had shared them with me back when I was still finding my way! When you know how to visualize, enhance positivity, use dream boards, practice affirmations and see how the Law of Attraction is working all around you, you're in a wonderful place to start making the kinds of changes you've always wanted to see in your life.

I sincerely hope that you've enjoyed reading about some of the major ideas, exercises, techniques and thoughts that have helped me so much. Remember, all of these suggestions are designed to inspire you, so please feel free to come up with your own unique spin on each technique! As you get used to using these approaches to daily living, it will become easier and easier to know how little tweaks and changes might help you tap into your positive side even more quickly and powerfully.

However, I want to emphasize that if you want to learn even more about the Law of Attraction, there are plentiful opportunities for further growth. This really is just the beginning, if you want it to be. You may already have seen dramatic changes just from adapting your everyday habits in the ways I have suggested, but that there is so much more to the story! When you have a sense that you've mastered the techniques in this book and are feeling confident about your use of the Law of Attraction, one of the best things you can do is to consider moving on to my "Origins" program. As I mentioned, some of the most important and exciting aspects of the program concern the science and techniques related to the true nature of the Intention Point. This is something I've discussed in fairly abstract terms in the foregoing chapters, and which I truly believe represents the difference between trying and failing to manifest. If you feel ready, join me there and learn how to access, shift and understand your Intention point. I can't wait to meet you at the next stage of your journey! In the meantime, I trust that you've learned enough to start creating wonderful new opportunities for meaningful change. I wish you all the happiness, love, and abundance I know you deserve.

Continue your journey here:

www.thelawofattraction.com/learn-about-origins/

64314911R00040

Made in the USA
Middletown, DE
11 February 2018